ZENOBIA

ZENOBIA
The Curious Book of Business

A Tale of Triumph Over
Yes-Men, Cynics, Hedgers,
and Other Corporate Killjoys

Matthew Emmens *and* **Beth Kephart**

BERRETT-KOEHLER PUBLISHERS, INC.
San Francisco

Berrett-Koehler Publishers, Inc.
235 Montgomery Street, Suite 650
San Francisco, CA 94104-2916
Tel: (415) 288-0260   Fax: (415) 362-2512   www.bkconnection.com

Ordering Information
Quantity sales. Special discounts are available on quantity purchases by corporations, associations, and others. For details, contact the "Special Sales Department" at the Berrett-Koehler address above.

Individual sales. Berrett-Koehler publications are available through most bookstores. They can also be ordered directly from Berrett-Koehler: Tel: (800) 929-2929; Fax: (802) 864-7626; www.bkconnection.com.

Orders for college textbook/course adoption use. Please contact Berrett-Koehler: Tel: (800) 929-2929; Fax: (802) 864-7626.

Orders by U.S. trade bookstores and wholesalers. Please contact Ingram Publisher Services: Tel: (800) 509-4887; Fax: (800) 838-1149; E-mail: customer.service@ingrampublisherservices.com; or visit www.ingram publisher services.com/Ordering for details about electronic ordering.

Berrett-Koehler and the BK logo are registered trademarks of Berrett-Koehler Publishers, Inc.

Printed in the United States of America

Berrett-Koehler books are printed on long-lasting acid-free paper. When it is available, we choose paper that has been manufactured by environmen-tally responsible processes. These may include using trees grown in sus-tainable forests, incorporating recycled paper, minimizing chlorine in bleaching, or recycling the energy produced at the paper mill.

Library of Congress Cataloging-in-Publication Data
Emmens, Matthew, 1951-
  Zenobia : the curious book of business / Matthew Emmens and Beth Kephart.
  —1st ed.
    p. cm.
  ISBN 978-1-57675-478-8 (acid-free paper)
  1. Business–Fiction. I. Kephart, Beth. II. Title.
  PR6105.M57Z34   2008
  823'.92—dc22   2007037669

FIRST EDITION
13 12 11 10 09 08   10 9 8 7 6 5 4 3 2 1

To all those who make it their business to see past what is, toward what must be

CONTENTS

PREFACE

What is Zenobia?

Is it a strange place? Is it a prescription? A simple fantasy?

Certainly those seeking a series of straightforward steps to business success would do better to journey elsewhere, for Zenobia is a place of twists and turns, unexpected encounters and surprise. Certainly those who depend on politics and hierarchy to propel their careers to a "higher" place won't find any of that here.

Zenobia is, instead, for people who recognize that corporate life is very much an adventure—a place where the imagination can open the most extraordinary doors. It's for people who dare to assert their own best thinking where they work and who dare to let their business environment stir positive change within them.

I've spent more than thirty years in business, working my way through its various channels as a sales representative, a marketing manager, and a senior executive. I've spent time at established multinationals like Merck & Co., and I've had the privilege of helping to launch wholly new organizations such as Astra Merck and EMD Pharmaceuticals. Throughout it all I've observed that the people who are most successful at what they do are the ones who embrace the wild rise and fall of the adventure—who find energy in risk, opportunity in the unknown, and possibility in the people all around them. Those who succeed compete with their colleagues, not against them. They view their organizations not as overwhelming, impersonal, implacable forces but as places where they have the chance to influence positive outcomes. They recognize that, while companies are defined by market value, earnings per share, assets, processes, and intellectual property, succeeding rests in the hands of people.

Success is not an absolute measure; it's the goal each employee sets for himself or herself. Those who succeed name their objectives and then seek out a path—asking for help where they need help, leveraging the expertise of others, and choosing to lead by their own example, no matter where they are "ranked," no matter how they are titled. Those who succeed are not afraid to bring their true human selves to the job every day—their talents, their anxieties, their pride, their toil, their determination, their humility, their empathy for others, their willingness to take on challenges, assume risks, push beyond known boundaries, and, most importantly, believe in something that is not yet there. Those who succeed aren't afraid to fail, for failure is only, in the end, a chance to grow and learn.

Adventure stories have the rub of the familiar about them; we read them to our children and we remember having had them read to us. In their pages we meet those rousing heroes and heroines who face scary obstacles and take memorable risks while encountering enemies and finding unexpected allies. We learn again that fears must be overcome if the extraordinary is to be achieved, and by the end of these tales, the extraordinary usually happens. Adventure stories have been told for eons. So why have we failed to apply them to business?

Zenobia: The Curious Book of Business is designed to take you on an adventure—to transport you to a place where even the most crumbling structures and stubborn personalities are transformed by the enthusiasm, conviction, and courage of the story's heroine. What is strange here will quite quickly become familiar. It will, we hope, inspire you to change the way you view your own world of work—to take what already is and transform it into what must be. For only the creative and the courageous can lead change. Only passion can turn ruin into rightness and transform work itself into something more like fun.

Zenobia is a mythical place, a place where the heroine's adventure becomes a pathway to success for others. It is, as well, a mystical place—a place that reminds us all that one's own success can be achieved only when others succeed as well.

Curious indeed.

Matthew Emmens
Wayne, Pennsylvania
January 2008

Now I shall tell of the city of Zenobia, which is wonderful in this fashion: though set on dry terrain it stands on high pilings, and the houses are of bamboo and zinc, with many platforms and balconies placed on stilts at various heights, crossing one another, linked by ladders and hanging sidewalks, surmounted by cone-roofed belvederes, barrels storing water, weather vanes, jutting pulleys, and fish poles, and cranes.

Italo Calvino, *Invisible Cities*

1

MAKE OF THE UNKNOWN
AN ADVENTURE

There was, to begin, no apparent way up. The doors of the elevators had been sealed long ago. The stairs zinged this way and that, crossed over and through, circled back and endlessly in. Some enterprising soul had thrown a ladder up, but it was perched at a delirious angle. Someone had tried to launch a lavender kite, but its tail sagged sadly around the balustrade. There were precarious rope bridges tethered across the atrium. There were tunnels threaded east and also north. There were doors that were locked, there were rooms with no lights, there were windows blackened over, sealed shut. Hardly ever did the old phones ring. At Zenobia there was trouble.

"Excuse me," Moira said, for she was new to this place and she had only just now made her way from

her car, across the moat, to the guard at the turnstile.
"How do I find room 133A?" She was wearing red
shoes and a neat woolen dress. She was thinking about
something her sister once said: *No one has ever seen a
black hole straight on. The evidence has forever been
entirely indirect.* Moira always remembered her sister's best instructions at opportune times, for her sister
was an astronomer who knew darkness as well as light.

"Room 133A?" repeated the guard, after mulling the
question for a surprising stretch. "Room 133A follows
132B and precedes 135C. And just for the record,
there's no 134 nor, to my knowledge, a 135A or B. But
that last part is just between you and me," he said, lowering his voice. "Tell no one that I told you."

Moira pushed her round glasses up the bridge of
her nose, flipped back her bangs, and took in the
scene—the ropey overpasses and crooked stairs, the
forlorn kite tail, the smudge-colored tunnels. Arrows
pointed in a thousand directions, but there was no
way of divining their meaning. For whom had those
arrows been hung and painted? Moira wondered. And
when? It seemed to her to be some kind of code, the
sort of thing a lucky archeologist might find in a pre-
historic cave.

"But which way," Moira said, hoping to be clearer this time, "might I go to find room 133A?"

"I've told you enough," the guard said sulkily, as if he'd been asked that question a thousand times before. "Much more than enough for one day."

Moira glanced at her watch. It was 8:10. The classified ad that had brought her to this place had presented but two key instructions: find room 133A and arrive no later than 9:00 a.m. That was it—no interview, no references, no vetting of her credentials—just a time and a room number. She had recently left a job that had bored her to tears. She had promised herself an adventure. This sounds appealingly odd, she had said to herself. But odd is one thing, somewhat mild. Zenobia, so far, was quite strange. Nevertheless, she boldly entered—through the turnstile, straight into the atrium.

"Thanks for your help," Moira told the guard, and, reluctantly, he buzzed her in. Taking a left, Moira started walking. This would be, she decided, like finding her way through the night. And she had practice at that, the sort of grit that comes from years of persevering. She had, with glasses on, the keenest pair of eyes. She could see through mess and muddle. She could see what wasn't there.

2

TAKE CARE, LEST YOUR SUCCESS LEAD TO RUIN

How long had it been like this—always threatening to rain? How long had Zenobia been the color of smog and mud? Long ago, Zenobians had taken to dressing for the gloomiest of weather, and the fashion had prevailed. They had taken to their jobs as if taking to chores—reacting and surrendering and sighing to themselves, keeping their eyes in a miserable squint. The place had lost its sense of humor. It had no zeal, no passion.

Here's what would happen to any idea that got suggested: it would be ignored, snuffed out, or flattened. Here's what Zenobians thought about risk: not here, not now, not ever. Here's how Zenobians would go about their days: with blinders on and chins tucked in, with one eye on the clock. Revenues, of course, were flat. Profits were perpetually falling. Not an ounce of polish was on any surface. Innovation was the purest abstraction.

From where he sat, in his room above it all, Gallagher appraised and contemplated. He had the thick, white hair of a seasoned man but the physical grace of a former athlete—a gymnast, perhaps, or a tennis player. He'd been with Zenobia through its heady days of ascent and also during the miracle of its heyday. He'd thought, at one point, that he'd make it into one of the clubs, but to him the doors were never opened. He'd been good old Gallagher, reliable old Gallagher, when-you-need-something-fixed-go-to-Gallagher Gallagher. He'd been passed over time and again but always gently. *We need you where you are, old boy. You shift, and we all crumble.* He'd put off his wife, who wanted him to come home, who pointed out, almost every night, that his colleagues were off on perpetual vacations and that other wives, married to other husbands, were having a whole lot more fun in their lives.

Stubborn, increasingly isolated, Gallagher proffered initiatives that had advanced precisely nothing. His attempt to lift the stultifying strictures had deepened

6

the prevailing paranoia. His suggestion that the executives who had not yet parachuted out convene to chart a course for the future had been rebuffed. Gallagher's memos on change had gone unread. He found copies of them scattered in trash cans. Once he brought in a spare kite from home and looped it around a tarnished railing, the kite being suggestive to him of the bold and serendipitous, the kite being— maybe?—an inspiration. But if anyone had caught wind of it, they hadn't been inspired. They'd all gone around with their eyes cast down, with their shoe soles thin, in their treacherous trench coat fashions.

"Retire," Gallagher's wife kept pressing. "Please. Come home and start a garden. Why give yourself away to those who cannot know what you are giving? What is the point of wanting a change when no one wants the change with you? What is the purpose of your heroism, Gallagher, when no one's taking notice from above?"

3

CONCEIVE A PLAN; PURSUE IT

The first man Moira encountered inside was very tall and very thin; his eyes were shards of black beneath thick eyebrows, and in one hand he grasped a bundle of file folders. His lips were moving but emitting no words. He wouldn't have even noticed Moira had she not stopped him with a question.

"Excuse me," she said, "but could you tell me how to get to room 133A?"

"Room 133A," said the man. "I've heard of that." He shifted his folders from the one hand to the other, rubbed his chin, reversed the folders, then straightened himself around his long spine, as if preparing to go. Was he actually, Moira wondered, going to walk away? No, Moira thought, he absolutely couldn't, and so she decided to detain him. She stepped a little closer and peered into his eyes.

"Moira," she introduced herself.

"Hedger," he mumbled.

"Should I go this way?" Moira asked, pointing east, toward the tunnels. "Or up and around, over those stairs, toward the bridge?" Not wanting to appear demanding, she added pleasantly, "If you would be so kind as to tell me."

"My suggestion," Hedger replied, after more apparent conversation with himself, "is to go whichever way your predecessor went. If you think that's right. Maybe it's so."

"I have no idea," Moira said, taken slightly aback, "who my predecessor was or if there even was one."

"How unfortunate," Hedger said, looking genuinely pained. "One does what's always been done; that's the way we get on. Or not. I'm afraid I won't be able to help you. At least right now. But perhaps later?" Behind his glasses, Hedger's eyes were pinched. He took a perfunctory look at his watch.

"I think," Moira said, "that I'll try the west wing first."

"I'd caution against that," Hedger said, "since you've never been there."

"Nothing ventured," Moira said, "nothing gained." It was one of her sister's favorite borrowed wisdoms and never anything shy of supremely useful.

"I've calculated the risks," Hedger confided, "and there are many. You could lose your footing. You could fall. You could be in for a gross humiliation. And at the end of it all, you might not find what you came for. You could go miles and miles, all for nothing."

"Better than going nowhere, don't you think?" Moira asked, remembering herself all those years ago in the grip of scotophobia—those palpitations, that slurry speech, the way she shook when it grew dark, for that was what she was afraid of: shadows. She'd had to go to sleep before the sun set so that she would not feel the encroachment of shadows. She'd had to call for her sister in the middle of the night, whenever she woke with her heart in her throat. No bats hung on the ceiling, her sister had assured her. No ghosts hid in the shadows. The lights beyond the window were stars, not eyes. The closet was just a closet and not a door to outer space.

Moira's sister had made Moira get up and maneuver through the dark for herself so that she might eventually see. She had made her come to terms with the night for there was no other choice; the night would always be there. She had told Moira about all the other people who had once been afraid and who were no more, who had chosen to face whatever challenge head on rather than to live a life of elaborate evasions. Though it had taken Moira years to beat the fear, she had emerged from all that battling a changed person. She'd crawled through a tunnel to the other side— moved forward and more forward until she'd acquired a certain pluck. *You remind me of me*, her sister had lately been saying, and nothing could ever make Moira any prouder than to be compared to this person she both idolized and loved.

"I don't suppose room 133A is going to come looking for me," Moira said after a while. "It's up to me to find it."

"But you're a woman," Hedger said.

Moira shrugged. "So?"

"It'll be harder for you. The risks are greater."

Moira looked at Hedger and his long, anemic face and did not say what she was thinking. Then she looked beyond him—at all the unconstructed chaos of Zenobia, the diverting stairs, the thick rope swing, the kite in the ironwork of the railing. No net would catch her were she to fall. There is no implicit promise in adventure save that something will happen, something new will be lived.

"I have this sister," Moira said, "an astronomer sister, who says that darkness is adorned with light."

"A ridiculous inversion," Hedger replied. "Unscientific."

"Growing up I aspired to be like her," Moira said. "To see beyond what is, toward what might be. To make patterns out of chaos. To be at ease with the unknown." Moira looked down at her shoes, as if they might hold some answer.

"Red," Hedger said, following her gaze, "is awfully brazen."

"You've been of such little help," Moira said as politely as she could.

"True," Hedger said, only vaguely affronted, "but don't come looking for me when you're lost."

"Wouldn't dream of it," said Moira.

"So where will you go, then?" asked Hedger.

"I have an idea," Moira said. "I plan to test it."

4

CELEBRATE DIFFERENCES, OR WATCH THEM BREED DISTRUST

It hadn't always been this way. For a time, Zenobia had stood among the mighty—productive, efficient, effective—an exemplar. Its widgets were unlike any other widgets. Its people boasted sterling résumés. T-shirts and baseball caps and office mugs and coolers were all emblazoned with the single word *Zenobia*, a word synonymous with prestige and power.

But power had become a drug. Rather than continuing to lead the market forward, Zenobia had come to believe that it was, itself, the market. Rather than asking the question, Is our business self-sustaining? Zenobians had begun to obsess over their personal legacies. Artificial rituals for inclusion in the top management echelon had become the norm—there was the Ivy League Club, the All-Male Golfing Squad, the

Twenty-Years-of-Service Elite. The smug and the myopic had replaced the pioneer. Distrust shadowed every conversation, delusions were endemic, and not only weren't the right risks taken, the right risks weren't ever identified.

Those who stayed spent excessive time defending their own turfs. Level Sevens would dismiss the work of Level Sixes, only to present that work as their own, a few days later, to panels of Level Eights. Level Nines had perfected the art of the curtailed conversation—of declaring themselves late for another appointment whenever a decision had to be made or an apology rendered or a simple question answered. Level Fours made certain that Level Threes didn't get copied on memos that might have given them some insight. Level Twos circumvented Level Threes in open bids for big promotions. Level Fives refused to team with Level Fives for fear of being shown up, pressed, or challenged. Level Sixes hid behind the work of vendors.

Agendas were rewritten to keep key issues off the table. Employees were criticized for having élan. Gossip became gospel. Differences became distrust. Decisions of dubious merit were made in fits of abominable self-interest.

For a couple of years, Zenobia's defenses had held strong. A team of lawyers had safeguarded its widget patent. The company had taken up residence inside a moated fortress. Employee rules had kept employees in check. Widgets shipped out; revenues shipped in.

But fissures become cracks and, subsequently, gaping holes. Snags become tears. Angst becomes disillusionment, and the marketplace is not a company; it's a dynamic. A new flight of competitors was making itself known, making widgets inspired by customer needs, taking business from Zenobia. The leaders of Zenobia had no vision for the future. One by one, they parachuted out. Bought their golf condos and yachts. Left behind an irrelevant architecture that could only serve another, distant time.

The vast majority of Zenobians had given up— worked off checklists, took dictation, stopped asking other people questions, then stopped asking questions of themselves. Every other Friday, no matter what they had or had not contributed, they all left the place with their paychecks.

5

PREPARE FOR RIDICULE

She'd scuffed her shoes a bit on the coarse, uneven risers. The big rope swing hadn't wanted to budge. Freeing it had taken all she had. The slatted wood bridge chattered, but everything in the end had held, and she had not looked down, which had helped. Moira touched her bangs with the tips of her fingers. She straightened her dress, dusted dust from her shoes. Here we are, she said to herself. Here I am, and that is progress.

At the entrance to the west wing, Moira paused and took a deep breath before walking on ahead. She was glad for her flat shoes, enormously so, for here in the west wing the floor was all angles and ramps, inclines and mostly declines—everything jimmied up and wedged together, made-to-fit but hardly. Amidst the bifurcated ramps were countless drab-green cubicles, like so many brussels sprouts attached to a stalk. An ambient hum filled the room, emanating from the banked bulbs above, and any window light that might have existed had been pirated by the perimeter officers that lay, sluglike, behind closed doors.

To Moira's dismay, she could see no room numbers nor even any names assigned to any workspace. There were labels only, brassy anonymous indicators of levels. There were far more Level Ones than Level Twos, Moira discerned, as she, increasingly curious, wandered about. Far more Level Twos than Level Threes. And after she'd walked around and around until even her flat shoes were pinching, she could attest (had someone wanted her to attest) to having located but four Level Sevens, two Level Eights, and a single Level Nine. What a mixed-up place this is turning out to be, Moira thought. The artificial lights hummed monotonously above. She felt a knob of pain in her right temple and heard the words of her sister in her ear: *Constellations are the way we humans have of giving the masses of stars above some logic.*

Just then Moira's thought was diverted by the squeak of a cart that was headed, mercifully, in her direction. Ordinarily the squeal of poorly oiled wheels and the grating bleat of machinery would have set her on edge, but here, bedeviled by monotony, she found the clamor reassuring. The cart, for its part, was like nothing she'd ever seen—a whirligig of whirring parts. She noted cartridges of ink, reams of paper, and a profusion of slots, and in the very center of this whiz-bang contraption sat a rolling, ink-glossed drum (brown ink, Moira noted, corporate brown). It seemed entirely medieval and grotesquely new wave at the same time, and as she stopped to study it, Moira began to understand that the equipment came with its own human attendant—a delivery person who was not just maneuvering the cart but also tending to its multitude of pieces.

Though she was by now just footsteps from this man and his contraption, Moira had managed to go unnoticed. It seemed wisest, then, to watch and listen— and so, taking advantage of the attendant's apparent myopia, Moira took in the peculiar scene. When the attendant pressed a button, Moira noted, the inked drum rotated left, seized a blank piece of paper with its notched teeth, rotated some more and rotated again, then released the newly printed page into a shiny white tray beneath an artificial sunlamp. Once dry, the communiqué was maneuvered through a slot

and delivered, by means of some invisible forces, to the mail bins that were pinned on the outside wall of every office—the whole operation taking far more time to describe than to complete and the mail bins themselves hardly being the end of the story, for up through each mail bin shot a human hand, which snatched the communiqué and then disappeared.

Moira watched the whirligig make three or four deliveries. She watched the hands as they snatched and vanished. At last her presence was divined by the attendant. He seemed to notice her shoes first, and then her knees, then returned his stare to her candied-apple-colored shoes, which clearly were, in this man's eyes, Moira's most alarming feature. A born disciplinarian, the man shook his rather-on-the-large-side head and clucked his tongue.

"Are those within our branding guidelines?" he asked Moira, rubbing an ear with one hand and gesturing to her shoes with the other.

"Well, I don't know," Moira answered. "I've just arrived."

"Fascinating," the man said. "I should say."

"It would be a lot more fascinating," Moira ventured, "if I could find room 133A."

"I bet it would," the man said, still studying the red of Moira's shoes and tsking a little for effect.

"Those were my instructions," Moira said. "Room 133A."

"What if I told you," the man said, "that you are the fourth person who has come trolling for room 133A in the past month alone and the very first of the crowd with red shoes?"

"What happened to the others?" Moira asked, feeling her heart quicken and demurely (she hoped) placing one foot behind the other.

"They gave up," the man reported of the others. "They didn't make the grade." He delivered the news without sympathy or judgment. It was a matter of fact, and it stuck.

Had the others tried hard? Moira wondered. Had they been given any help? Had they searched every wing, ramp, and planky corridor? She wanted to ask but changed the subject instead, saying, most politely, "I've never seen a machine like the one you've got there. It's quite a work of art, I suppose?"

"It's the What and the How," the man offered freely. "And I'm Bolt." Moira could practically see the capitalized nouns as he spoke. "Daily Directions. Every Level getting its own Daily Task List, as prepared by the

Level above. It's how we do business," he continued. "It is," and here he articulated most grandiloquently, "how business gets done. Our very own unique process, cultivated over years and then some. It would take me hours to explain it," the man said. "And in the end you wouldn't understand it because I'm the only one who does." This was a man who was proud beyond proud. This sort of gloating had its own most burnished shine.

"What if something unexpected comes up?" Moira wanted to know, touching one finger to the machine, feeling its hum.

"It never does," said Bolt and then continued, unprompted: "We make sure of that."

"But what if one What negates the significance of another? Or one How doesn't always work or could be better? Or say somebody finishes all his tasks before noon? What does he do for the rest of the day?"

"Not here," Bolt said. "Couldn't happen."

"Are there separate instructions for teams?" Moira inquired. "A stash of instructions in a file somewhere to accommodate new strategies or visions, a sudden change in weather?"

"Teaming," Bolt tsked, "is entirely too talky. Too many possible miscues. Too many fights. And

change—haven't you heard?—is a misery. We do as little of that as we possibly can. We excel at the familiar."

"You're not a big fan of serendipity, I take it," Moira
said, not openly declaiming, not yet.

"Serendipity is neither economical," he answered,
"nor efficient. Indeed," and here he lowered his voice,
"we avoid the unknown at all costs. The unknown is
such a fickle thing. It can make one look so . . . foolish."

Just then a swoosh of Zenobians appeared at the
crest of the ramp where Moira and the man were
standing. They were headed, it seemed, for the room
just beyond, a break room; Moira smelled coffee. One
had feet that made the loudest of sounds—pound-
pound, pound-pound on the carpet. Another bore an
impossible grin. The third had a lascivious-looking
tie—a geometry of browns, each brown more muddy
than the next.

"Hello, Bolt," they said, while to Moira they said
nothing.

"Hello, Stomper and Nod and Vert," he rejoined,
and then to Moira he mumbled, "Excuse me." Pushing
and pulling and persuading his machine, he soon
joined the others in the break room. Moira felt sud-
denly stranded and strange. She stayed right where
she was. She didn't move.

It wasn't long before she heard the kind of din that used to scare her in the middle of dark nights—screeching, scratching, scattered coughing. It was a second after that when she came to understand that the screeching was all about her.

"When will these people learn?" Vert snorted.

"Room 133A," Stomper said. "As if."

"But the red shoes are precious," Vert blurted. "You've got to give her props for the red shoes."

"Give her props for the red shoes," said Nod.

"We should steal the shoes," declared Vert. "See what that does to her homing instincts."

"If I haven't found 133A, then she'll never find 133A," snorted Stomper. "It's all just as simple as that."

"Think about it," Vert said. "We take the shoes and we toss them somewhere. Then we watch her flounder."

"The point is, we ask her to leave," Stomper went on, for he never did hear what anyone else was saying. He was, perhaps, physically incapable, his ears being the size of a baby rat's nose.

"You let me know if I can help," Nod offered.

"When I want help, I ask for help," said Vert.

"Yes you do," said Nod. "Absolutely."

The word *serendipity*, it seemed, was a very funny word. *Teaming* was a hiccough. Stomper had a lot to say about paths he'd forged and things he knew and the impossible naivety of those who broadcast difference.

"Must have had some strange growing-up years, that girl," he chuckled.

"Probably played by her lonesome on the old elementary school yard," said Nod.

"Yeah," said Vert, "and never got to her senior prom."

"Who in the world," asked Nod, "would ask her?"

"Bet she got only teachers to sign her yearbook."

"Come on," said Stomper. "She's not worth the endless time in our entirely endless days."

Moira felt the burn of some kind of shame in her cheeks. She stood frozen where she was, despairing over her choice of shoes and ruing her decision to leave her last job. For wasn't boring better than this? Didn't doing nothing compare favorably to inciting a riot of ridicule?

Maybe, Moira thought, it was her time to leave. Maybe this was a stupid enterprise. Maybe who cares if she finds room 133A? There are plenty of other companies, she thought, and most aren't spilling sideways and spun together with hooks and swings and ladders. Most aren't so riddled with so much spoiled humanity.

Maybe I don't belong.

But then Moira remembered one of those long, dark nights when the wind had started to blow. She'd thought the sound at her window was the sound of something bad, but it was only the tapping of tree limbs. Beyond the sound, however, was a strange green-blue light, a wavering fabric of color that had so alarmed Moira that she had cried out—one quick, bursting shout.

Her sister had come at once to her rescue. She had stood beside Moira at the windowsill, looking out to the wild lights beyond. *An aurora borealis*, she had explained, getting a look on her face that Moira knew she'd not forget—a look so purely full of appreciation that slowly, slowly, Moira began to breathe. Moira had asked what an aurora really was. Her sister had said, *A collision of atoms.* Moira had suggested that the congregated colors in the sky looked like a visitation by the haunted. Her sister had said that it was all in the seeing. *I see curtains,* she had said. *I see magnificent striations. I see a show put on for those of us who choose to see it.*

Moira had a choice, in other words. To see nothing in Zenobia but ignorance and failure. Or to see, amidst all the ruin, the sparks of possibility. Heroines are never meek, Moira reminded herself. Heroines are not cowed by mediocrity.

6

KNOW THE WORLD WILL CHANGE, DESPITE OR BECAUSE OF YOU

One day as Gallagher watered the jasmine on his office windowsill (his wife having foisted the plant upon him), he caught sight of something irresistible in the streets below. Autumn had recently yielded to winter, and it was nearly dusk. Along the main boulevard, a crowd had gathered—old people and young ones, people wearing red and people wearing white, people who wore their hair cropped close and those who boasted the most extravagant braids. Some among them were very short and some very tall. Some were very quiet and some couldn't stop talking. Some were dressed as if for a formal affair, while others had holes in their jeans and thinned-out patches on their sleeves. But the interesting thing was how homogenous they seemed, how vested with cohesion and intent upon some dream.

Gallagher had opened his window to get a better look. He had leaned in the direction of the crowd. It was hard to make out just what was being undertaken at first, but slowly Gallagher had come to understand. Lanterns of light were being lifted into trees—hung among the boughs of pines and spruces. The heights of people, their fashions, their clothes seemed to dictate where they stood and what kind of lanterns they hung.

The joy of it all was what struck Gallagher most deeply, the revelatory way these folks had of working together. Sometimes the taller people would lift the shorter ones to their shoulders, someone would offer a braid as a measuring stick, or someone would use his very small hands to nest a candle inside the lantern glass. After each lantern was hung and each candle secured, the crowd would honor what had been completed. Even as the skies grew dark, no one ever stopped to check the time.

Finally, when it seemed that every lantern had been hung, a golden-skinned woman stepped out from the crowd. Words that Gallagher couldn't hear

were spoken, and in response the crowd built itself into human scaffolding—hands clasping hands, knees bent deep, men and women stooped so that their backs were as flat as tabletops. When the scaffolding was in place and its joints found to be true, the golden-skinned woman began to make her climb. In her right hand, she had a calibrated stick that sizzled at its tip with fire. Lantern by lantern, the candles were lit, until a word had been spelled among the trees.

Now the human scaffolding broke apart and the crowd began to mold itself into a sturdy semicircle. From its center stepped a youngish man who carried with him a bright bubble lantern. Purposefully he strode toward the first pine in the sequence, where the lanterns formed a single vertical. Leaving just enough space above this column of light, the man then hung his own lantern. He moved his head from side to side, appraised, made an adjustment.

Then he reached into the lantern and touched its candlewick with one extenuated finger. The dot above the *i* burst magnificently to life—a brilliant, practically effervescent color that completed the lit word: *imagine.*

7

LOOK FOR WHAT COULD BE, NOT JUST WHAT IS

It was something, Moira thought as she made her way down the ramp and away from the noise of the break room, to encounter a succession of people so seemingly devoted to maintaining the status quo. She sniffled a little and dabbed at her eye. Surely the guard knew more than he was letting on. Surely Hedger didn't really believe in standing still. Surely Bolt had generated a communiqué, at one time or another, from or to or relating to the elusive room 133A. Surely Vert wouldn't take her red shoes. Could he be as mean as that? Was stealing at Zenobia somehow legal?

What had become clear to Moira was that she and her quest lay outside the norm—neither were recognized entities in a world lavishly devoted to entrenched conventions. Zenobia wasn't just twists and turns and levels and lists. It was also a sound—the sound of static and gossip and envy, the sound of anything but progress.

Still, the place had a history. It couldn't have always been like this. Someone had to have built the ladders and hung the rope swing. Someone had to have thought to lace a kite into the balustrade. There must have been others who had yearned to get somewhere, who had traced out a new path from here to there. What this place seemed to be lacking most of all was connections—not just between parts but between people. She noted activity across the atrium. Carefully, very carefully, she made her way. She was breathless and also untidy. The watch on her wrist read 8:35.

By now she was in one of the tunnels leading toward the east wing, headed down and down and up, through darkness. She dragged one hand along the tunnel wall to stave off disorientation and pushed her glasses up the bridge of her nose in a vain but noble attempt to get a clearer glimpse of her surroundings. She saw at last the proverbial light at the end of the proverbial tunnel. And heard noise. The clatter and click of nails on keys. The *brrrr* of copiers and printers. The high-pitched complaint of a fax machine. Civilization, Moira thought, which was odd, as she was, after all, still standing in a tunnel in a company called Zenobia that was hardly, by so many standards, civilized.

Still, the east wing seemed populated by an early shift, by people, Moira discovered, who were already at work above the steam of their coffee. The east wing had no pretense of offices or cubicles. Instead, the cavernous space was chockablock with workstations that looked like Moira's middle-school library carrels—narrow desks with half-height dividers that separated one workspace from another. In the somber light, the computers glowed. The letters and symbols were like so many phosphorescent worms crawling across the screens.

Everybody, Moira noticed, was facing east, their backs hunched in permanent unease. On every head was a pair of headphones, making it easy for Moira (whose eyes were now altogether dry) to step forward unnoticed and take a closer look at the work that was so determinedly getting done. PowerPoint slides, Moira said to herself. Everyone at work on PowerPoint slides. And the closer Moira looked, the better she understood that the subject matter, screen to screen, was eerily comparable—regurgitations, statistical and otherwise. Department by department, budget by budget, sales record by sales record, warehouse by warehouse, Zenobia was being PowerPointed. It was being put into columns and marched out into rows, and every template Moira saw was titled What Was, while every screen was the dullest gray.

Please, Moira thought, let there be something more than meets the eye in this. Please tell me that all these people don't spend the entirety of their workday lives reconfiguring old data. She walked and she walked until she found screens whose color was not gray but blue and whose templates were titled What Is. But that was all Moira found: far more history than present tense. Nothing planned for the future.

What collective story, Moira longed to ask, were the PowerPointers telling? How could all these rows and columns add up to narrative? The business of business is ultimately people, not numbers, Moira knew—people working together, ideas sometimes colliding, one person's suggestion becoming the basis for a group possibility. It's about provocation and convergence—even Moira knew that. And yet on all these screens were but fragments.

It was already, Moira realized, 8:42. Her job at the moment was to find room 133A, and toward that goal she had made no progress. "Excuse me," she said, tapping a nearby woman on the shoulder, "but I've been trying to find a certain room, and so far I've come up empty."

The pale-skinned woman had yellow hair that seemed to be painted into place. Her fingernails were filed straight across and lacquered the blackest black. She seemed not to have understood Moira's question, for she removed her headphones, rubbed one ear, and simply said, "Trenchy. And you?"

"Moira," Moira said.

"Odd name," Trenchy opined.

Rolling her eyes, Moira persisted. "I need someone or something," she rephrased the refrain of her question, "that can give me the lay of this land, who can direct me to room 133A."

"All I've got here," Trenchy said, shaking her headset at Moira as if it were some kind of jingle bell, "is what I'm told. Anything else is speculation."

"No map?" Moira tried not to sound like she was pleading. "No floor plan? No general overview?"

"I take dictation," Trenchy said. "Nothing more." She smiled and Moira noted the slightest gap between her two front teeth. Moira noted again how pale Trenchy was, how sunless in general was the room, how black were those lacquered fingernails. If you turned off the fluorescents it would almost be dark. But that didn't throw Moira.

"Would any of your colleagues know?" Moira pressed, sweeping her hand toward the ranks of hunched backs.

"I have no idea what my colleagues know," she answered. "They having their work, and me having mine."

"How about your supervisor, then?" Moira asked, trying not to get dizzy.

"That person," Trenchy said, "works on another floor."

"Ever heard of room 133A?" Moira asked, but not because she expected an answer.

"You're funnier than you look," Trenchy said. "Funnier even than your name. A little crazy, too, if you ask me."

"I guess I'm on my own," said Moira.

"A lot of good that's done you so far," Trenchy said, fitting her headphones to her head. She looked at Moira in the way that declares a conversation finished and then added, "And when you don't find room 133A, don't claim that I didn't warn you."

How utterly unhelpful, Moira thought. How terribly stale. She moved on, and now as she pressed on, she thought of all she had to prove—not just to herself but to all Zenobia.

8

STEP BEYOND YOUR WALLS TO FIND YOUR WAY

It was after that—after *imagine* had been lanterned into a stand of evergreens—that Gallagher once and for all determined that there'd be no changing Zenobia from within. The catalyst would have to come from someone or some ones who had energy, spunk, a little derring-do, the ability and desire to outwit, outthink, outdream most any kind of roadblock. "Help wanted," Gallagher wanted to shout out from his window to the bustle below. But he fashioned a classified ad instead:

> **WANTED:** Someone capable of finding his or her own way while leading others. Creative persistence a prerequisite. A desire for the extraordinary an absolute must. Some gleam would be good. No references required. Report to room 133A. Arrive by 9 a.m.

Gallagher placed the ad in newspapers, magazines, and fliers; he paid for billboard space and told not a soul what he had done. Then he painted the door to his office red, watered the jasmine his wife had foisted upon him, and, with a rising sense of anticipation, set himself to waiting. Change need not always come from the outside, he knew. But right now, right at this moment, Zenobia was desperate for a jolt.

9

LISTEN WELL

It took Moira less time to find her way out of the tunnel than it had taken to find her way in, and when she arrived back at the central core she discovered that the building had grown far more densely populated. Zenobians were making their way to wherever they went, to do the work they were accustomed to doing. They either ignored her or gave her odd stares as she passed. Some pointed their fingers quite rudely.

Moira watched as the employees navigated the stairs, unlocked a few doors, and began filling some rooms with dim light. Despite the mess of things, the men and women proceeded in matter-of-fact fashion—favoring that one big swing, that one wooden bridge, that one set of stairs and primary corridor, that single set of branching hallways. Wherever the carpet had already been worn down to threads, wherever the handrails had changed color from the touch of so many palms, wherever there were countless scuff marks and scars, wherever the ropes were frayed— that's where Zenobians were headed.

The rest of the building sighed with disuse. The kite tail sagged. The ladder slumped. The rope bridge seemed to doubt itself. The tightrope was frayed. Moira thought of her sister's favorite poet and favorite poem. Visionaries, Moira emboldened herself, take the road less taken. Wherever the others were going, Moira would not. Wherever others had not been, some kind of future hovered. That was Moira's conviction, at any rate, for what was the point in bemoaning the mess? The point was to solve the riddle, to find the singular zigzag of handholds, levers, and platforms that could take her spiraling up, toward the atrium's highest height, where something bright red and promising shone in the far, but attainable, distance. She mapped out a plan that began with that kite tail, which would propel her, she decided, to a ladder. The ladder itself led to that precarious tightrope. The tightrope twisted and curled toward that red. Moira had to get to the tightrope first. And then she had to demonstrate the most immaculate balance.

Thank goodness, Moira thought, for her sensible shoes, for she had to take a running start to leap toward the kite tail. It was all air for a nanosecond, and then she had the kite tail in her hands. She was holding on and swinging forward so that she might fly toward the ladder. Her glasses had slid to the very tip of her nose. The wind was in her face. It was scary. *Sometimes fear is a choice you can choose not to make*, her sister had taught her. But still.

Moira pushed and pumped and pulled with her legs. She closed her eyes and focused on momentum. When at last she blinked her eyes open again she saw a handful of Zenobians pointing up in her direction. Worse, she saw one of them near the worn balustrade, making a grotesque mockery: the woman had pulled her thickly rimmed glasses to the end of her freckled nose and was twisting her arms around an imaginary kite tail. She was grunting like maybe Moira had been grunting, and it was embarrassing and gross and also awful.

"What's your name?" Moira called out to her.

"Killjoy," the woman said and then giggled.

Someday she'll think me a genius, Moira told herself now, swinging closer and closer to the ladder. She closed her eyes. She was resolved. She wasn't paying heed to a couple of small-minded insults.

"That woman's certifiable," said another mimicking man, whose proper name was Snort.

"What's it to you?" someone said. "Mind your own business."

"Excuse me," returned Snort. "But I don't recall asking you for an opinion."

You're fine, Moira told herself. Truly you're fine. Though her hands had begun to slip, and if she didn't soon propel herself to the crooked ladder, she would surely tumble—tumble through the air, tumble into shame, tumble from whatever grace she might still muster. She remembered one night with her sister, explaining that the floor in her room was a trap door, that she couldn't get up and walk around because she would fall and fall. *You can't believe that*, her sister had said. Why not? Moira had asked her. *Because if you do you'll live out your life in the confines of a bed.* I'm afraid of falling, Moira had protested. *You should be more afraid of going nowhere*, her sister had said.

From down below, Moira heard someone suggest that she point her toes to give herself momentum, and because nothing else was working, Moira did. And now a man was talking about grip, telling Moira not to ride so high on the tail, to loosen her fingers, change her angle, and Moira listened. She pointed her toes and she altered her angle. She was swinging faster now, and further.

"Can you believe this, Nod?" she heard Snort say. "They're egging her on, as if she'll make it."

"Ridiculous," said Nod. "Absolutely."

"If you hit her feet with a stick, you could rattle off those shoes," proffered Vert. "What do you say, Wizzy, huh? You think a stick will do it?"

"That isn't an idea," the man who must have been Wizzy answered. "That's simple treachery."

"And what have your own ideas done for us lately? Is Zenobia any better because of you?"

"You're old news, Vert," puffed Wizzy. "Once you figure out where the front door is, it'll be closing behind you."

"For goodness' sake," and now it was the tut-tutting voice of Bolt. "According to the schedule, we should all be working. There'll be consequences if we don't—frightful consequences." Where in the world had Bolt come from, Moira wondered? Shouldn't he be delivering communiqués? And more to the point, shouldn't he, out of plain old-fashioned humanness, be offering to save her from her plight? What was wrong with all these people? Why couldn't they think past themselves?

"How uneducated do you have to be," said someone who sounded—distressingly—like Stomper, "to put your faith in the tail of a kite?"

Not uneducated, Moira thought. Not stupid either. And not ready to give up her shoes. Just swinging and swinging and swinging and swinging and pointing her toes and trying to rouse up some height. She was out of reach, at last, of the dreadful Vert. She was starting (but just barely) to feel all right. She was two swings away from reaching the ladder's first rung, and then she opened her hands and went flying. She soared through the air; her hair blew with the breeze. She reached out her hands for the ladder. One down, Moira thought. A ladder's climb and a tightrope's walk to go. And then that red something in the distance.

"Well done," someone said, waving a hand in her direction. It was an enthusiast, the sort of person one needed just then. I will thank her, Moira decided, when I'm done.

"It was like watching arabesques," opined Wizzy, with a respectful sigh.

"I told you she'd make it," Nod said, with all the confidence of a man who actually believed what he now was saying.

"Make it where? To some old broken ladder?" It was Snort again, Moira just knew it. She heard Stomper and also Vert: "Girl's gone absolutely nowhere worth going." "When will they learn? Or will they?"

Then, from Bolt: "We are off script. We are off time. We are supposed to be working."

Moira was breathless and flushed and her hair was a mess. She was shocked, but then she shouldn't have been. If she was going to have an impact on others, then she had better eradicate, once and for all, this feeling of being surprised by herself.

Moira took a hard look at her next challenge while she waited for her heart to calm. She looked at the lobby and the ceiling, at the hecklers and the enthusiasts, at the doubters and the believers, and thought about the nature of her mission and the uncertainty of the outcome. The ladder to which she now clung was even more warped and misshapen than she'd thought it would be when she'd first appraised it

from a distance. Entire rungs were missing at unfortunate intervals, and in many places the wood was so
bowed that the overall effect was that of a poorly writ-
ten letter. There would be no straightforward going on
this. She'd need to make careful leaps and steady
stretches. In some instances, she'd have to operate
blind.

Onward, she urged herself. Because people are
watching. Because she had something to prove—not
just to whomever was watching but to herself as well.
She had wanted an adventure, but was she up to this?
She had believed herself cured of her fear of the dark,
but dark comes in a thousand different shades, and
this was something new.

Little by little she began to make her way. In some
places, she had to walk the rungs with her hands, as if
performing a monkey-bar routine. In other instances,
she found herself crawling laterally, parallel to the
atrium floor too far below. Where the ladder snaked,
she snaked with it. Where it went up straight, she
planted her feet and stretched. Sometimes she had to
lean backwards and grab at supports she could not
see, and this—well, this was dangerous—and increasingly, warmingly, some people in the crowd saw her

through. The more Moira looked as if she might succeed, the more she was joined in her quest.

"A little to your left," Moira would hear someone call out to her. "No, a bit too far. Go right again." From the corner of one eye, she would see somebody waving. She would see furrowed brows on people leaning over the rail and squinting as if staring into the sun.

"Keep your chin up," she'd hear. Or "You're making progress. You are extremely brave. Take a little breather. There's a rough patch up ahead."

As tired as her overly extended limbs had grown, as tough as all the going was, as much as the woman who hated Moira's shoes wouldn't keep her opinions to herself, Moira found herself feeling oddly buoyant. Zenobians were helping her! One of the men in the crowd knew a lot about leverage. Someone else seemed particularly good at mathematics—at calculating the risk differential between respective alternative moves. And then there was a woman whose specialty, Moira concluded at one particularly difficult juncture, was something that felt like faith.

And through it all Moira listened for what was useful. She filtered out all that was not. She made her way up and over and through, to the end of the ladder,

toward the tightrope, above a thickening crowd.
Room 133A, she said to herself. And she understood
that the room wasn't just some job but a rooting-in
place that might—and wasn't there always this
chance?—sustain her going forward.

10

YIELD NOTHING TO THOSE WHO CAN'T SEE PAST THEMSELVES

The first job applicant to arrive at the Zenobia gates was a rather wiry man with a gleaming pate. He had the pointiest elbows Gallagher had ever seen and a style Gallagher read at once as bluster. The man had timed his arrival for 8:59 a.m., as if banking on a simple expedition. That isn't verve, Gallagher had thought to himself when he saw the man; that's more like arrogance.

At the gate, the man was announcing himself with a haughty, hasty flourish. "I'm what you've been waiting for," Artless declared to the guard, without the slightest hint of irony.

"Fascinating," mumbled the guard, barely lifting his eyes from the morning's Sudoku puzzle.

"The ad says 'wanted,'" Artless persisted, brandishing a folded copy of a newspaper. "I'm to report to room 133A."

"Maybe so," said the guard, for it made no difference to him. "But I didn't place the ad, so it's not my problem."

"I'm just asking for directions," Artless pressed.

"Never been there," the guard said. "Never had cause to go." The guard was no more going to assist the stranger in his quest than he was going to engage in an out-and-out confrontation. Zenobia was Zenobia. He was there to safeguard it, not explain it. He kept the strangers out, he let the old crowd in, he opened the door just this wide when someone obviously very new had a pass or proven purpose. Besides, this morning's Sudoku puzzle was much too special, and Artless's presumption was unworthy. "Have a good one," said the guard, as he buzzed Artless in. He looked up briefly, then returned all thoughts to his puzzle.

"But it's almost 9 o'clock," the man implored. That was the word for it: imploring.

"And so it is," said the guard, with a shrug. "So it is."

In the atrium, Artless rubbed his head and took a few embittered steps forward. Gallagher tried to put himself in the man's too-shiny shoes—tried to imagine seeing the place with fresh eyes. The swerving architecture and creaking connections, the slatted over-head bridges and unwieldy ramps. Tunnels and stairs emanated in countless directions, and nothing, but nothing, obeyed the laws of the perpendicular.

"What a flipping mess," Artless said, directing his words to no one now and throwing his long arms out in despair. He began to walk around and around in one unproductive circle—he circled the atrium, went up one ramp, poked his head inside a tunnel and then retreated—demanding of anyone he happened to encounter that he be shown the way. He wanted respect, but he'd done nothing to earn it. He wanted help, but he did not know how to ask. He wanted to lead, but before he could do that, he had to try to see, to try to find his way, to look for signs, to take some chances.

He wasn't having any of that. Zenobians were having nothing of him. Five after nine, and just like that he was gone, declaring to the guard on his way out that Zenobians didn't know squat about squat nor did they know what they were missing.

A few days passed before the next applicant appeared, and this time she was beseechingly pleasant—that much could be told from any distance. Even as she leaned toward the guard and asked for his help, this woman didn't remove her round and very rosy-colored glasses. "Oh, look at this now," Gallagher heard the woman say to the guard. "Isn't this a most intriguing space?"

Gallagher saw the guard raise his head and look beyond the woman, toward the atrium, where, yes, the dust was still hanging and the stairs were still splitting and the tunnels were menacingly dark. The guard scratched his head. It was the same dilapidated, disorienting Zenobia as the day before, and when he turned back to study the woman, Gallagher could tell he was a little confused. "Intriguing?" asked the guard. "Maybe you need a new prescription for those glasses."

"I've always had these glasses," Fog Hilda said, not in the least bit offended. "They suit me just fine. But thank you."

"Can I help you?" the guard prompted, in a bald attempt to move the woman on or out.

"Room 133A," Fog Hilda said. "I'm to report there."

Gallagher saw a shudder of recognition pass over the guard—a smidgeon of interest where before there'd been none. "Is that a fact?" he said.

"It is a fact," Fog Hilda said. "And I love facts, don't you?"

"When you can find them, they're good, I guess," said the guard. "Though most facts are fickle."

"What about room 133A?" asked Fog Hilda. "Can you tell me about that?"

"Just that it's here somewhere. Off," the guard said, pointing ambiguously toward the atrium, "in that direction."

"You've been so helpful," Fog Hilda assured him, bustling away toward nothing she'd ever be able to navigate. The guard smirked and shrugged his shoulders, letting the woman through without another word.

It was 8:45. The lobby had its fair cross section of people—some with their noses buried in the files they carried, some with their noses in the air, some benignly carrying out routines they had stopped questioning years before. Fog Hilda made it her business to encourage each one as he or she went by: "Good morning," she said. "What a lovely place." It was as if she were depending on her cheer alone to light her way to room 133A. As if she'd confused optimism with naivety, one springing from a way of looking at the world, the other from not looking at the world closely enough. As if she thought the job of a leader was to deliver good news, but oh, Gallagher thought, she was mistaken. Leaders watch, leaders study, leaders know

where there's trouble. They understand the root of it and work toward a cure. As many kind words as Fog Hilda threw out to passersby, they got her nowhere. She, like Artless, kept walking round and round, in and out and in again, until she walked straight out the front door.

A few weeks later a man showed up at Zenobia's door dressed in the finest sportswear. He had running shoes and a nylon tracksuit; a stopwatch hung about his neck. The guard, by now, was onto this. "Room 133A?" he asked the man before the man could ask it of him. "Room 133A?" he asked again, when he got no answer.

But the man didn't stop—didn't seem to see much need to. He went from walking to sprinting to leaping in a matter of seconds. He hurdled high and long over the guard and his gate, landed in the atrium and kept on sprinting. "You've got to be kidding me," the guard mumbled. Then he turned and watched, just as Gallagher sat up high and watched, to see what would happen next. Both knew the man would get nowhere. Neither feared an incursion.

Imagine an Olympic hurdler and a very fine horse all wrapped up into one—a creature capable of leaping every obstacle set before it with unflagging energy and style. That was the spectacle Hurdler put on, a phenomenal show of athleticism if ever there was one. Any balustrade, any bridge, any broken-toothed stair, any anything this man would leap. He could and would do it all, but after a while it got extremely dizzying.

This man, Gallagher soon realized, had no plan. Or, rather, his plan was unidimensional; it was to leap and to leap—to persist, if you will, but this persistence was anything but creative. It wasn't strategic, it wasn't thought through, it was impulsive and ultimately to no end. And all the while the man amassed a crowd—Zenobians who found him either alarming or amusing, who understood, without a soul saying so, that the man was all for one, and that one was himself. What had started out looking like capacity was quickly devolving into a circus act—a sideshow and distraction.

After a while, it seemed that Hurdler got bored. He persisted until persisting held no charm. Then he took one more sprint toward the jaw-dropped guard and leaped toward the world beyond.

How depressing, Gallagher thought. The perfect example of hideous self-absorption.

11

SEEK THE UNLIKELY
ALLIANCE

S tanding where she was, on the final rung of the
ladder, above the heads of a spiraling crowd,
Moira felt a little swoosh move through her and then
regained her balance. Slowly she turned toward the
tightrope. "Oh, dear," she sighed quietly. "What was I
thinking?"

For yes, she'd gotten far, and yes, a crowd was
watching, and yes, she'd have a thing or two to say to
the told-you-soers down below, to Vert, wherever he'd
gone off to. But once again she'd have to propel herself to the next part of the journey. She'd have to leap
from the ladder to the rope, and she was high, high,
high in the air, and for all the progress she'd made in
her battle against the dark, for all the pluck she had
carried forward in her life, for all the faith she was

placing in this journey, she had to admit that she had never really mastered the art of walking a straight line, and walking a straight line was what was now required most. Moira felt her throat constricting and her mouth going terribly dry.

"Didn't I warn you?" cried out Stomper, so anxious by now for Moira to fail, for if she didn't, Stomper would be wrong.

"You can do it," the enthusiast countered. "Don't listen to him."

But as a matter of fact, this wouldn't be easy. Yes, Moira knew that long ago the Chinese had tightrope walked over knives. And yes, once a man named Jean Francois Gravelet had both cooked and consumed an omelet while standing on a wire strung across Niagara Falls. But Moira was, at the end of it all, only Moira, a recovered scotophobic, an ardent perseverer, a woman in search of a room. Could this be the end of her road? Could Snort be right? No, Moira thought. If nothing else, it had become her job to prove him and the other naysayers wrong.

It was then that Moira noticed the very tall man with the thick eyebrows who had been carrying, when she'd first met him, that much-too-large bundle of folders. The one who had been so abundantly

unhelpful just—what had it been?—some forty min-
utes ago. It was Hedger who had pressed himself
through the crowds, it seemed, so that he might stand at
the balcony. He was looking at Moira with the odd way
he had of looking. He appeared to be talking to himself.

"Are you still looking for room 133A?" Hedger finally directly asked her in that grating voice of his.

Defiantly, because something about Hedger made
Moira feel defiant, she answered, "Why, yes. Of course
I am."

"And you think you can get there by means of
these contraptions? By a kite tail, a ladder, a rope?"

The crowd had stilled like crowds will still when
something electric seems destined. Moira heard only
the creak of the ladder. Only the slightest of breezes
wafted by.

"I know where I'm *not* going," Moira said. "And
that's where everyone else has already gone."

"Hmmm," Hedger said. And again, "Hmmm. Hmmm.
So many risks. So very many dangers." He shifted the
bundle of folders in his hand. He gave her that look.
She sighed with theatrical exasperation. She would
have stomped her foot, if she weren't so precariously
dangled.

"Do you know what I've always done?" said Hedger, after a strained silence had passed between them, after no heckler had heckled, not even Stomper or Snort.

Here we go, Moira thought. More fearful cautions, more praise for history.

"I've thought about posture, being as tall as I am. I've thought about taking my spine for a walk, of always righting my center of mass." There was a strained silence. "I merely thought," he said, when Moira didn't answer, "that I would pass that along. If you insist on persisting, that is."

From her vantage point, Moira couldn't properly tell if she was being mocked, cautioned, or supported. This man could not be on her side, or could he? What was he trying to tell her—spine for a walk? center of mass?

She didn't know. It can be hard to tell your detractors from your allies—to distinguish between differences that are beneficial and differences that point the way to trouble. Maybe Hedger did know something Moira didn't. Maybe she should set aside her biases and listen. Maybe he was trying to help her even though he clearly didn't agree with the direction she was taking.

"What do you mean?" Moira finally said over the hush of the crowd that kept gathering. "Taking your spine for a walk?"

"It's all about weights and counterweights," Hedger tried to explain. "I'm naturally lopsided, so I've found that it helps to carry," he said as he lifted one hand, "this calibrated bundle of folders. It keeps things right with me."

"I've never thought about taking my spine for a walk," Moira said, feeling slightly less confrontational, perhaps even, though she wouldn't just then admit it, grateful. "I wouldn't know where to begin."

"I would begin with your shoes," Hedger offered, "for they might have gotten you this far, but on a rope like that, they'll likely slip, and then you'll slip with them. And, if you insist on going forward, I . . ."

"My shoes," Moira conceded, slipping her feet, one by one, out of each shoe and gingerly placing the pair on a nearby rung. They had served her well, these shoes, but now she was ready to go beyond where they could take her. "Good point."

"And then I'd encourage you to consider stretching your arms out wide, side to side, as if they were your very own balancing pole. Increases your rotational inertia," the man continued, "and on a tightrope that's a very good thing."

"My rotational inertia?"

"Yes. The point," Hedger tried to simplify, "is to keep your center of mass as squarely above the rope as you can."

"So that I can take my spine for a walk," she said.

"Yes. Thank you for listening. That's what I'm thinking."

"And this can actually be done?" she asked. (And was she testing him, or was she testing herself? At this point she wasn't precisely sure.)

"History provides plenty of examples," Hedger said. "I've researched and cross researched."

"Score one for history," Moira said. And realized that she meant it.

"But don't you look down," a blue-eyed lady chose this moment to chime in.

"Don't forget what you've accomplished so far," she encouraged.

"Say good-bye to Hollywood," said Stomper.

"We're here for you," another somebody promised.

"You're making it. You are."

But Moira couldn't stop to respond. She couldn't stop to assess. She had to give her all to focus. For this was it, and she was standing up.

And she was taking the leap.

And she was standing with both stockinged feet down on the rope.

And she was balancing with arms straight out and eyes straight ahead.

And she was taking her spine for a walk.

"Here's to room 133A," went up the cry from nearly all around.

Hold on, Moira thought. Just hold on.

But also, just keep going.

12

EMBRACE THE ARRIVAL OF THE NEW

Another week went by before any other applicants appeared at the gates of Zenobia. In the meantime, the guard had made ready. He'd done some asking around, he'd called up old electronic files, he placed a "Where is room 133A?" speech on tap, should such a thing prove necessary. So today, when a bespectacled young woman appeared wearing bright red shoes and a quizzical expression, Gallagher looked down and saw the guard smile. Gallagher smiled himself. Change, he thought, is incremental.

"Excuse me," Gallagher heard this young lady say. She was polite, Gallagher noted, but refreshingly firm. "How do I find room 133A?"

"Room 133A?" repeated the guard with what might only be called officious delight—the delight of having an answer, of being ready. "Room 133A follows 132B and precedes 135C. And just for the record, there's no 134 nor, to my knowledge, a 135A or B. But that last part is just between you and me," he told this fourth applicant, lowering his voice. "Tell no one that I told you."

Gallagher could see the red-shoed young lady push her round glasses up the bridge of her nose, straighten her bangs, and take in the scene. He could see her sigh, then harden with determination. Nibbling at her lower lip, she persisted.

"But which way," she asked the guard, "might I go to find room 133A?"

So pleased had the guard been with his newly acquired bevy of knowledge, his on-tap speech, that the young lady's further inquiry threw him into something of a pout. He'd come up short, the guard had—however politely, the young lady had made this clear—and that was enough to put him into a sulk. "I've told you enough," he declared. "Much more than enough for one day."

Gallagher glanced at his watch. It was 8:10. This young lady, he thought, has not arrived with presumptions. She is not wearing running shoes. Her glasses are not tinted pink. This could be interesting. The guard buzzed the eager applicant in. She turned and thanked him for his help.

For whatever reasons she might have had, the young lady took a left and started walking—up and down until she found her first interior Zenobian—an old-timer named Hedger who had never progressed far through the ranks. Gallagher could hear but some of what went on between them as the applicant asked and the old-timer listened, then proffered advice that didn't sit right with the girl. Gallagher understood that she was asking again—restating her question, taking a new tack—but her interviewee would not be budged from whatever guidance he was giving. The exchange left Red Shoes flabbergasted but determined. I like this one, Gallagher found himself thinking. This young lady has promise. Ever more intently, Gallagher watched as the young woman escorted herself through the quagmire that was Zenobia—as she studied every sign and forged a path. She was, it seemed to Gallagher, sensationally spry—alert to possibilities, unafraid to take risks, aware of what she did not know but not intimidated by the challenge. She swung on swings, she tiptoed over bridges, she turned down corridors, and she traveled over ramps, all the while listening and looking and considering, accepting nothing at face value, not yielding to the noise of naysayers, the doubts of bystanders, the grind of smarmy envy. After she'd made her way past the What and the How and tunneled toward the PowerPointers, after she'd asked questions and listened and sorted wheat from chaff, she had become, in Gallagher's mind, a woman who would not be thwarted. She would traverse every corridor, swing on every rope, keep looking. She was on the hunt for room 133A, and this young lady in red shoes was going to find it. A small seed of optimism had started to sprout, and Gallagher felt impatient with hope. He felt expectant, and that was both odd and reassuring.

Do you know how jasmine grows its tendrils long and wreathes its leaves into circles? That's what the plant on Gallagher's sill began, just then, to do. Do you know how a breeze blown through an open window will carry the outside in? The air in Gallagher's office gleamed.

Down below, meanwhile, the young woman had drawn a crowd. She had started to ascend—to climb and swing and tiptoe and twist her way up the broken corkscrew of the ladder that she had reached—even Gallagher didn't know precisely how—by flying on the silk of a kite tail. It was outstanding.

It was nothing, increasingly, that she could do alone, for now in places she had to climb blind, she had to ask for help and trust it, she had to not listen to the people who made it their passion to stand in her way. The atrium crowd kept getting bigger, encircling her like an outstretched hand. The noise was everywhere as calls went out, one over and after the other, suggesting maneuvers and tactics, goading the young lady forward and onward and upward or telling her that she couldn't do it. Out of the chaos a matrix was being forged of the most unimaginably disparate parts, and ever increasingly, she climbed. She adjusted her glasses. She called out a breathless thank-you. She understood that she was not alone in her bid to find room 133A.

For Gallagher, it was no longer enough merely to bear witness. He wanted—he had to—participate, too. He wanted to help, somehow to ease the trail, to pay honor to the verve of this young lady. From his closet he pulled a bucket of red paint and a brush and quickly freshened his office door. Then he snipped some of the jasmine and with it made a wreath and to the wreath he added apples that he'd picked the day before from a tree limb near his window. Then Gallagher pushed the door even more ajar so that Miss

Red Shoes, if she finally reached the threshold, would feel more than welcome there.

13

INVENT YOUR
OWN FUTURE

The monstrous challenge of the Zenobia tightrope was that it curlicued. It went all around like a big corkscrew before it looped out and up. Moira felt like she was walking a succession of bicycle wheels, but she never looked down and she kept her arms out straight, and over the heads of a murmuring crowd she kept on going. Oh, how she longed for a glass of water. Oh, how she ached. Oh, how much scarier any of this was than finding her way through the dark. There was, she began to see, a door up ahead—an end, perhaps, in sight. She had no idea what time it was. She no longer thought it mattered. She no longer thought herself new to this place. She felt as if she'd been a Zenobian for years.

Later she would say that she was changed forever by the air she found up there, by the way everything about her sparkled. What had been dust now appeared to be light—countless scintillas of amber, ocher, and rose, an aurora borealis of sorts. It was like standing inside her sister's most farseeing telescope. It was like telling someone she loved a dream. She wanted to move forward and more forward, reel effortlessly through light. She wanted to live this and imbibe it, always to remember and never forget.

"It's gorgeous up here," she heard herself saying, her eyes straight ahead, her arms out. "It's all the colors of the sun, dispersed in fragments." But no, that wasn't the half of it, that wasn't even the truth, yet how indeed could she ever explain it? And was explaining even the point? she wondered. Could reporting back or summarizing ever do this journey justice? Wasn't her journey a collective achievement, and shouldn't the end now be shared?

"It's not that hard," Moira began to speak louder, still not looking down, still holding her balance. "Start with the kite tail," she said. "Then take the leap. Think of taking your spine for a walk."

But instead of being greeted with an exuberant hurrah, Moira heard a strange and stilling silence. Have

I climbed too high to be seen? she wondered. Can anything I say up here be heard? Do they all think that I've gone crazy? She couldn't look down now. She simply had to speak louder. "Invent your own future," she called more forcefully.

Finally, out from all that sudden silence, she heard an answering voice—Trenchy, the woman with the painted yellow hair: "Are you suggesting that we join you?" she asked, her voice somewhere between temerity and fear. "That we come to where you are?"

"I am," Moira cried out, her optimism returning in one exuberant rush. "This is the risk worth taking."

"But there's only one room 133A," Hedger said. "Only room for one of you."

"Look around," Moira insisted. "What do you see? Plenty of opportunities like this one."

"You only did it because you're new," said Snort; Moira recognized that voice in an instant. "I could have done that, too, ten years ago."

"I did it because I tried," Moira said. "Because I kept my eyes open. Because I wouldn't be thwarted by the likes of you."

"Arrogance," Snort huffed, "will get you nowhere."

"You shouldn't be messing with irony," Moira said. "It doesn't really suit you."

"Don't try to confuse me, Miss Miss," Snort said. "You won, you achieved. Isn't that enough?"

"If I achieve, we all achieve. Don't you get that, Snort?"

She was trembling, for she had reached a difficult juncture in her own tightrope walk. She was persevering because this mattered, because anyone at all can leap and sail and climb and balance if she manages to lose her fear and look beyond the moment. "Think momentum," she exhorted them, even as she silently exhorted herself. "And leverage. And stretch until you can stretch no more. And find a point on which to focus amidst all the din."

The door, Moira realized, was coming into view. It was looming nearer and nearer as she cycled down and cycled up. She had to concentrate. The door was bright red and had a pretty peaked roof, a wreath of jasmine and apples, and a slender gold mail slot, and the closer Moira got, the clearer it became that the door had been left slightly ajar. Her heart was pounding harder than it had ever pounded before. The pain in her right temple was forgotten. Snort was history. Vert was a loser. I'm almost there, she said to herself. Almost. And almost. And nearly nearly.

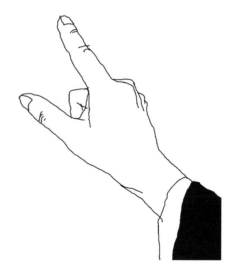

And how she wanted to call out to those below, how she wanted to tell them, how she knew that she should not look down. But she was close now and she had dared before and daring had served her well. So she held her breath and took one small glance back, over her shoulder, toward the path that she had taken.

What she saw just then was even far more dazzling than the lambent atmosphere. For at the end of the kite tail, on the rungs of the ladder, in the spaces between things, against the warp of wood, she saw a rising stream of Zenobians. Some were being carried on the shoulders of others. Some were arrayed in human chains. One was helping another remove a pair of heeled boots, and two had formed a bridge across which Trenchy was walking. Hedger was giving lessons on the center of mass. The man who knew grip was teaching grip. The woman who calculated risks was calculating. Bolt was distributing tips, the guard had left his desk and was applying muscle, and just like that, and altogether, they were moving forward, moving along.

They were making the journey for and with one another, showing each other the way. And those Zenobians who didn't join in were looking very small.

They were looking like has-beeners look, like what-wasers and not what-will-bes.

Hello, Zenobia, Moira said to herself. And hello room 133A. And that's when she heard the sound of music from behind the bright, wreathed door.

14

HONOR THE IMAGINATION

I thought," Moira said after a moment, for she was breathless, and the skin of her hands was split in places, and her feet had long since lost their shoes, "that I would never get here."

"But you did," Gallagher said, "and with aplomb." He was standing tall and his hair was lustrous. She was rubbing some dust from her knees, some smudges from her elbows, something from between the lashes of one eyelid.

"I did it with them," Moira said, gesturing to the threshold of room 133A and indicating the Zenobians beyond, many of whom were now following in her footsteps, bridging one another from ladder rung to ladder rung in every conceivable, most glorious fashion. "Or at least," she corrected herself, "with some of them." Moira dabbed her eyes a little as she spoke. She was overcome, and that was natural enough. Leaders are but human, after all. "I'm Moira," she said after a moment.

"Gallagher," Gallagher said, extending his hand. "And this, of course, is room 133A."

"Lovely," she said. "If a little out of the way."

"Well," he said, taking a quick look around. "I suppose it seemed that way."

"I saw many things," she said, "while I was on my way. Unforgettable things, really. Life lessons. But honestly, this was quite the journey. Unprecedented, to be honest, in my career."

"I was watching," Gallagher admitted. "I had the perfect bird's-eye view."

"Then you know," Moira said.

"Then I know . . . ?"

"Some of the troubles I had."

"We certainly have characters," Gallagher said, "at Zenobia."

"I had my share of detractors," Moira blushed.

"But you got people talking," Gallagher said.

"Some of them, anyway."

"And working together."

"I guess so."

"You got them wanting something new."

"Maybe they'd just forgotten that new was still a possibility. Maybe all I was, was a reminder."

"A catalyst," Gallagher corrected.

"If you say so," Moira looked at him and smiled. "Though I'm guessing the change began with you."

"It was just an ad," Gallagher said.

"It was an idea," Moira corrected. "An activated optimism. Which around here," now Moira smiled again and almost laughed, "must have taken considerable fortitude."

"There are still a million things to do," Gallagher said, stepping back and rubbing his chin.

"I suspect so."

"No changes for change's sake but lots of things that must be changed."

"Beginning with . . . ?" Moira asked.

"We'll have to decide what Zenobia is and why— name its truest purpose, elevate its differentiating qualities, build frameworks within which the right decisions can be fairly made. Our architecture will have to change. Our technologies. Our conventions and conversations. Our hierarchies. We should begin, perhaps, with a group exercise—the crafting, by all Zenobia employees, of want ads that describe the job they feel they should be in, the change they want to help create."

"I vote for retiring the What and the How," Moira said. "It's a machine," she explained, not knowing for sure if Gallagher had ever seen it.

"Vote acknowledged."

"I vote for a new fleet of PowerPointers in charge of What Will Be."

"But let's retire their technology. Give them something new to plan with."

"I would suggest personality training for the Killjoys and the Verts, the Stompers and the Snorts."

"There are those," Gallagher said, "who specialize in that."

"I vote for windows everywhere—operable ones that open onto the world beyond."

"Speaking of windows," Gallagher said, "do you want to see something extraordinary?" He took Moira by the hand toward his own open window and encouraged her to look out and see. The word that had been lanterned into the evergreens burned bright. The one word, still aflame with potential.

"Imagine," Moira said, reading what she found there.

"Yes," Gallagher said. "Imagine." And then they both turned toward the wreathed red door, through which winds of change had already begun to blow.

ACKNOWLEDGMENTS

I wish to thank Lois Veeder, for her support, and my three children, who are becoming so many things that I myself could never be capable of.

—Matt Emmens

Deep gratitude to our earliest readers—Anita Graham, Mike Cola, and Barbara Deptula—for their smart insights, and to Diane Evans. Thanks as well to manuscript reviewers Deborah Nikkel, Tobin O'Donnell, Allan Paulson, and Barbara Schultz, for investing their time and their passion. Thanks to Moira Moody, for the spark of inspiration and to Nettie Hartsock, for her Texas smarts. Thank you to Bob Harrell, who jumped right in and contributed so fully. We have been supported by an extraordinary team at Berrett-Koehler— the sharp editorial eye of Johanna Vondeling, the sweeping perspective of Jeevan Sivasubramaniam, the enthusiasm and talents of María Jesús Aguiló and Catherine Lengronne, the design expertise of Dianne Platner and Richard Wilson, and the deep commitment of the entire marketing and publicity team. We found our way to Berrett-Koehler via Beth's longtime, always wonderful agent, Amy Rennert. We received a thorough and much-appreciated reading from Robin Buchanan. And we were graced, most of all, by the phenomenal art of Beth's husband, William Sulit, who brought the book to life as only he could.

—Matt Emmens and Beth Kephart

ABOUT THE AUTHORS AND THE ILLUSTRATOR

Matthew Emmens began his career in international pharmaceuticals with Merck & Co., Inc., in 1974. There he held a wide range of sales, marketing, and administrative positions before volunteering in 1992 to help establish Astra Merck, the joint venture between Merck and Astra AB of Sweden. He later became president and chief executive officer. In 1999 he joined Merck KGaA and established EMD Pharmaceuticals, the company's U.S. prescription pharmaceutical business. Subsequently, he was promoted to president of the global prescription business and lived in Germany. In 2003, he joined Shire Pharmaceuticals as chief executive officer and member of the board. As CEO of Shire, Emmens has engineered an extraordinary revitalization, transforming Shire into one of the top specialty pharmaceutical companies in the world in just a few years' time.

Beth Kephart is the award-winning author of five memoirs and a partner in Fusion Communications, a company that collaborates with leading U.S. companies on the creation of special publications. She was a 1997 Pennsylvania Council on the Arts fiction grant winner, a 1998 National Book Award finalist, a 2000 winner of a National Endowment for the Arts grant, a winner of a 2005 Pew Fellowship in the Arts grant, and a winner of the 2005 Speakeasy Poetry Prize. Her work has appeared in the *New York Times*, *Washington Post*, *Chicago Tribune*, *Wall Street Journal Europe*, Salon .com, and elsewhere. Her sixth book, *Flow: The Life and Times of Philadelphia's Schuylkill River*, was published in the summer of 2007, and *Undercover*, her first novel for young adults, was recently released. Two more young adult novels are forthcoming. Please contact Beth Kephart through her blog, http://beth-kephart.blogspot.com.

William Sulit, who earned his graduate degree in architecture from Yale University, is an award-winning illustrator and a partner in the award-winning communications firm Fusion. For more information on Fusion, please visit www.fusion-communications.com.

Matthew Emmens and Beth Kephart have worked together for more than fifteen years.

ABOUT BERRETT-KOEHLER PUBLISHERS

Berrett-Koehler is an independent publisher dedicated to an ambitious mission: **Creating a World that Works for All.**

We believe that to truly create a better world, action is needed at all levels—individual, organizational, and societal. At the individual level, our publications help people align their lives with their values and with their aspirations for a better world. At the organizational level, our publications promote progressive leadership and management practices, socially responsible approaches to business, and humane and effective organizations. At the societal level, our publications advance social and economic justice, shared prosperity, sustainability, and new solutions to national and global issues.

A major theme of our publications is "Opening Up New Space." They challenge conventional thinking, introduce new ideas, and foster positive change. Their common quest is changing the underlying beliefs, mindsets, institutions, and structures that keep generating the same cycles of problems, no matter who our leaders are or what improvement programs we adopt.

We strive to practice what we preach—to operate our publishing company in line with the ideas in our books. At the core of our approach is stewardship, which we define as a deep sense of responsibility to administer the company for the benefit of all of our "stakeholder" groups: authors, customers, employees, investors, service providers, and the communities and environment around us.

We are grateful to the thousands of readers, authors, and other friends of the company who consider themselves to be part of the "BK Community." We hope that you, too, will join us in our mission.

BE CONNECTED

Visit Our Website

Go to www.bkconnection.com to read exclusive previews and excerpts of new books, find detailed information on all Berrett-Koehler titles and authors, browse subject-area libraries of books, and get special discounts.

Subscribe to Our Free E-Newsletter

Be the first to hear about new publications, special discount offers, exclusive articles, news about bestsellers, and more! Get on the list for our free e-newsletter by going to www.bkconnection.com.

Get Quantity Discounts

Berrett-Koehler books are available at quantity discounts for orders of ten or more copies. Please call us toll-free at (800) 929-2929 or email us at bkp.orders@aidcvt.com.

Host a Reading Group

For tips on how to form and carry on a book reading group in your workplace or community, see our website at www.bkconnection.com.

Join the BK Community

Thousands of readers of our books have become part of the "BK Community" by participating in events featuring our authors, reviewing draft manuscripts of forthcoming books, spreading the word about their favorite books, and supporting our publishing program in other ways. If you would like to join the BK Community, please contact us at bkcommunity @bkpub.com.